How Long To Microwave A Potato

Dedication

To my father. Thank you for teaching the love of cooking that you had for many years growing up. Thank You for the simple idea of this book when I was younger by saying, "Not many people know the simple forms of cooking. They don't even know how long to Microwave a potato".

Index

Breakfast

Appetizers

Soups & Sandwiches

Beef, Pork & Lamb

Chicken, Turkey, Duck

Fish & Seafood

Sides

Sauces

Dessert

Breakfast

Breakfast is to some the most important meal of the day, however most people are not blessed with being morning people. These easy to create recipes, you will be enjoying a delicious breakfast before the coffee's brewed. You will be able to enjoy every ones favorites eggs and bacon, French Toast, to frittatas

Page Number
5. 2 Minute Scrambled Eggs
6. 2 Minute French Toast In A Cup
7. Blueberry Flax Muffin
8. Breakfast Potatoes
9. Cinnamon Roll Mug Cake
10. Coffee Cup Coffeecake
11. Coffee Cup Quiche
12. French Toast Sandwich
13. Fruit & Granola Crisp w/ Yogurt
14. Granola Cereal Bar
15. Eggs and Bacon Sandwich
16. Huevos Rancheros
17. Eggs and Spinach Sandwich
18. Egg, Cheddar, & Avocado Sandwich
19. Oatmeal Bars
20. Omelet Sandwich
21. Zucchini Ham Frittata

2 Minute Scrambled Eggs

Ingredients

-2 Eggs
-2 Tbsp of Milk
-2 Tbsp Salt

Directions
-Coat Coffee Mug or Microwave Safe bowl with cooking spray. Beat Eggs, Milk and Salt til blended.
-Microwave on HIGH for 45 Seconds, Stir.
-Microwave on High til Eggs 30-45 Seconds til almost set
-Top with cheese. Salt & Pepper Optional

2 Minute French Toast In A Cup

Ingredients
-1-2 Slices of Bread, Cubed
-1tbp Butter
-1 Egg
-2 tbsp Milk
-Dash Cinnamon
-Drop of Vanilla Extract

Directions
-Cube Bread
-Melt Butter in Cup
-Add Bread to Cup
-In Separate bowl combine egg, milk, cinnamon, and vanilla. Stir
-Pour mixture over bread. Allow to soak
-Microwave 1 minute . Then 10 seconds more until you are satisfied

Blueberry Flax Muffin

Ingredients

-1 Oz Frozen Blueberries
-1/4 Cup Ground Flaxseed
-1/2 tsp Baking Powder
-2 Tbsp Sugar Free Pancake Syrup
-1/2 tsp Orange Zest
-1 Egg White
-1/2 tsp Nutmeg

Directions
- Mix Dry Ingredients
-Add Egg White, Syrup & Zest
-Oil Cup
-Pour Mixture into Coffee Cup
-Microwave 90 Seconds

Breakfast Potatoes

Ingredients
-2 Medium Potatoes, Peeled & Sliced
-1/4 Cup Sliced Onion
-1/4 tsp Salt
-1/8 tsp Pepper
¼ tsp Garlic Salt
¼ Cup Shredded Cheddar Cheese

Directions
-Coat 9 in Microwave Safe Plate with cooking spray
-Arrange potatoes, onion on plate, sprinkle seasoning on top, cover plate
-Microwave on HIGH 9-10 minutes, until potatoes are tender
-Add Cheese

Cinnamon Roll Mug Cake

Ingredients
- 2 Tbsp Apple Sauce
- 1 Tbsp Vegetable Oil
- 1 Tbsp Buttermilk
- 1/4 tsp Vanilla Extract
- 1/4 Cup +1 Tbsp All Purpose Flour
- 2 ½ Tbsp Light Brown Sugar
- 3/4 tsp Ground Cinnamon
- 1 Dash Nutmeg (Optional)
- 1/4 tsp baking powder
- 1/8 tsp salt

Cream Cheese Icing Recipe
- 1 Tbsp Cream Cheese
- 2 Tbsp Powdered Sugar
- 1 tsp Milk

Instructions
- Combine Cream Cheese Icing Ingredients together, whisk til smooth.
- Set Icing Aside
- Combine All Cinnamon Roll Ingredients together mix til smooth.
- Microwave Cinnamon Roll mixture on HIGH for 1 minute
- Microwave additional 15 seconds til fully cooked
- Add icing over top.
- Enjoy

Coffee Cup Coffeecake

Ingredients
- 3 tbsp Dark Brown Sugar, Divided
- 2 tbsp all purpose flour
- 1 Pinch + ¼ tsp Ground Cinnamon, Divided
- 2 tbsp Butter Softened, Divided
- 1 pinch Salt
- ½ Egg beaten, divided
- 2 tbsp Sour Cream
- 1 tsp maple syrup
- 2 drops vanilla extract
- ¼ Cup Self Rising Flour
- 1 tsp preserves

Directions
-To Make topping, combine 2 tbsp brown sugar, all purpose flour, 1 tbsp butter, pinch of cinnamon, & salt in small bowl. Mix together with fingers until crumbs form.

-To make batter, mix remaining butter & brown sugar together and mix til creamy. Add egg, sour cream, syrup & vanilla to bowl, beat until blended.
-Add self rising flour and remaining cinnamon, beat mixture til smooth.
-Pour half mixture into 12oz buttered mug, add preserve to center.
-Pour on remaining mixture & sprinkle with crumb topping.
-Microwave on HIGH until done 1 minute & 15 seconds.

Coffee Cup Quiche

Ingredients
-1 Egg
-1 ½ Tbsp Milk
-1 pinch salt
-1 pinch pepper
¼ of a Bagel or similar amount of french bread
-2 tsp cream cheese
-1/2 slice prosciutto or ham
-Thyme or chopped chives
-Dijon Mustard

Directions
-Beat egg, milk, salt, and pepper together in cup
-Tear bread into dime sized pieces; stir in
-Add cream cheese; stir in
-Tear Up Prosciutto or ham; stir in
-Sprinkle with thyme or chives
-Microwave on HIGH until done about 1 minute 10 second
-Garnish with Mustard and Chives

French Toast Sandwich

Ingredients
-2 slices Aunt Jemima French Toast
-2 eggs
-2 slices Bacon
-maple syrup
-cheese

Directions
-Microwave/ Toaster 2 Slices of Aunt Jemima French Toast
-Beat 2 eggs in bowl and microwave til firm
-Microwave Bacon
Assemble Sandwich, top with cheese. Add second slice of French Toast

Fruit & Granola Crisp w/ Yogurt

Ingredients
-1 Cups Fresh or Frozen Sliced Peaches
-1/4 Cup Fresh or Frozen Blueberries
-1 tbsp Hot Caramel Ice Cream Topping
-1 tbsp Granola
-1/2 Cups Low Fat Frozen Yogurt

Directions
-Add peaches & blueberries into bowl
-Top with caramel & granola.
-Microwave on HIGH until bubbly 1-2 minutes.
-Top with Frozen Yogurt

Granola Cereal Bars

*This Recipe makes 12 bars

Ingredients
-1/2 Cup Brown Sugar
-1/2 Cup Creamy Peanut Butter
-1/4 Cup Light Corn Syrup
-1 tsp Vanilla Extract
-2 Cups old fashioned oats
-1 ½ cup crisp rice cereal
-1/4 cup miniature chocolate chips

Directions
-Combine Brown Sugar, Peanut Butter, corn syrup, and Microwave on High for 2 minute.
-Stir in Vanilla, oats, & cereal.
-Fold in Chocolate Chips
-Press into 9 in square pan coated with cooking spray.
-Cool and Cut into Bars

Egg & Bacon Pita Pocket

Ingredients
-3 Egg Whites
-2 slices bacon
-Dash Salt
-Dash Pepper
-1 Pita Pocket
-1/4 cup Shredded Cheddar Cheese

Directions
-Combine eggs, salt, and pepper, scramble. Microwave 30 seconds til firm
-Microwave Bacon in accordance with package
-Tear up bacon into bowl and cheese. Mix well.
-Microwave Pita for 30 seconds
-Stuff egg mixture into pita.

Huevos Rancheros Breakfast Sandwich

Ingredients
-2 English Mufins
1/3 Cup Refried Beans
-2 Eggs
-1 Ripe Avocado
-Salsa
-Salt
-Pepper

Directions
-Toast English Muffin
-Mash Up Avocado, add salt to taste,
-Microwave refried beans til warm & spread on bottom halves of muffins
-spread avocado mix to top halves of muffins
-Microwave eggs in bowl til cooked
-Add eggs to english muffin with beans
-Add Desired amount of Salsa
-Place Avocado seared muffin on top.

Egg and Spinach Breakfast Sandwich

Ingredients
-2 Slices Bread
-1 Large Egg
-¼ Cup Spinach (Chopped)
-1 Slice White Cheese
-1 tsp butter
-1 dash salt
-1 dash pepper

Directions

– Place slices of Bread in toaster, til slightly Brown
-Scramble eggs in bowl, add in salt, pepper, and spinach; whisk
-Microwave for 50 seconds. Flip eggs microwave additional 10 seconds
-Spread butter onto toast
-Add cheese slice
-Pour on eggs
-Top with other slice of toast

Microwave Egg Sandwich w/ Cheddar & Avocado

Ingredients

-Nonstick Vegetable spray
-2 large eggs
-1/8 tsp salt
-Pinch of Pepper
-2 tbsp shredded cheddar cheese
-2 slice toast, english muffin, biscuit, or roll
-1/4 avocado, sliced

Directions

-Spray Microwave safe bowl
-Add eggs, salt, pepper, and 1 tbsp water. Mix
-Microwave for 30 seconds. Stir Gently repeat, til eggs puff up
– Add cheese, til egg sets and cheese is melted
-Place Egg Mixture onto bottom piece of toast
-Top with Avocado, and other slice of toast

Oatmeal Bars

Ingredients

-2 Cups Quick Oats
-1/2 Cup Brown Sugar
-1/2 Cup Melted Butter
-1/4 Cup Corn Syrup
-1 Cup semisweet Chocolate Chips

Directions

-In large bowl combine oats, brown sugar, melted butter and corn syrup.
-Press into 9 in square microwave safe dish
-Microwave on HIGH for 1 ½ minutes, check on it. Repeat.
-Sprinkle on Chocolate Chips
-Microwave at 30% power for 4 ½ minutes or until chocolate is glossy.
-Spread chocolate evenly over top.
-Refrigerate 15-20 minutes.
-Cut & Serve

Microwave Omelet Sandwich

Ingredients
-2 eggs
-1/4 milk
-1/4 pepper; sliced
-1 mushroom; sliced
-3 strips microwaved bacon; torn up
-1 slice or shredded american cheese
-Diced green onion
-dash pepper
-2 slices Bread
-Butter

Directions
-Mix eggs and milk in bowl, add in cooked bacon pieces and vegetables
-Place bowl in microwave, cover with place and cook for 3 minutes
-Toast bread with butter
-Place omelet onto toast, cover with top slice

Zucchini Ham Frittata

Ingredients
-4 Cups Finely Chopped Zucchini
-1 small onion chopped
-4 large eggs
-3/4 tsp salt
-1/8 tsp pepper
-1 cup shredded cheddar cheese

-1 cup cubed ham

Directions

-In a Bowl combine zucchini and onion. Microwave, covered on high for 3-4 minutes. Drain
-Whisk eggs, salt, and pepper together, mix in cheese and ham.
-Poor over zucchini mix.
-Microwave at 70 % for 8-9 minutes or until center is firm

Appetizers & Snacks

Appetizers & Snacks are what make hosting meals with friends fun. Whether you are making these snacks for youself or to share with others, you will enjoy the taste as well as the ease that these simple dishes have to offer.

Page Number

23. Baked Pizza Taquitos
24. 5 Minute Hummus
25. Chili Cheese Dip
26. Cinnamon Caramel Apple Dip
27. Jalapeno Popper Dip
28. Pizza Dip
29. Sweet Potato Chips
30. Panko & Parmesan Topped Zucchini
31. Perfect Microwaved Nachos
32. Spinach Dip
33. Spicy Queso Dip
34. Cheesy Bean Dip

Baked Pizza Taquitos

Ingredients
-8 Soft Tortillas
-1/2 cup tomato sauce
-2 cups shredded mozzarella cheese
– 48 slices of pepperoni

Directions
-Spread 1 tbsp of tomato sauce on tortillas
-Sprinkle with shredded cheese
-Place 6 pepperoni slices in a line down the center
- Tightly roll tortilla and hold closed with toothpick if needed
-Repeat process
-Microwave on High for 1 ½ minutes, til tortilla has some crisp to it
- Serve with tomato sauce for dipping

Hummus

Ingredients
-1 15 ounce can of chick peas
-2-4 Cloves Garlic
-1/2 cup Tahini
-2 tbsp Fresh Lemon
-¾ tsp salt
-1-2 tbsp Extra Virgin Olive Oil

Directions
-Microwave chickpeas with liquid & whole garlic for 4-5 minutes
-Pour chickpeas, garlic, lemon juice, salt & tahini in blender.
-Blend until smooth and creamy, add olive oil during blending
-Add salt, lemon, or oil for taste blend til perfect

Chili Cheese Dip

Ingredients

-2 8 ounce packages of cream cheese
-15 ounce can of chili (favorite brand)
-2-3 cups shredded cheddar cheese
-Tortilla chips

Directions

-Spread cream cheese on the bottom of a microwave safe bowl
- Pour can of chili over cream cheese
- Sprinkle cheese on top
– Microwave for 5 minutes or until cheese is melted
-Serve while hot with chips

Cinnamon Caramel Apple Dip

Ingredients

-14oz Can Sweetened Condensed Milk
-1 Cup Butterscotch Toll House pieces
-2 tsp cinnamon

Directions
-Combine all ingredients in a glass bowl
-Microwave on HIGH for 1 minute
-Microwave in 30 second intervals stirring until melted
-Serve with sliced apple pieces

Jalapeno Popper Dip

Ingredients
-8 Oz Cream Cheese
-½ cup mayonnaise
-1/2 cup of sour cream
- ½ Cup Shredded Cheddar Cheese
-1/2 Cup Pepper Jack Cheese
-4 Oz can Diced Jalapeno Peppers

Directions
-Mix together cream cheese, mayonnaise, and sour cream until smooth
– Stir in Cheddar Cheese, Pepper Jack Cheese, and Jalapenos
Microwave for 3 minutes
-Sprinkle Cheddar Cheese on top let melt
-Serve with Bread, tortilla chips, of veggies

Pizza Dip

Ingredients

-8 Ounce Package Cream Cheese
-1/2 Cup Marinara Sauce
-1/2 Cup Chopped Pepperoni
½ Cup Shredded Mozzarella Cheese
-1 tbsp Parmesan Cheese
-1/2 tsp Italian Seasoning
-Option Diced Onion, Pepper, Mushroom

Directions
-Spread Cream Cheese into Glass Bowl
-Pour in Marinara Sauce
-Top with Pepperoni & Option Vegetables
-Sprinkle with Mozzarella Cheese
-Sprinkle on Parmesan Cheese & Italian Seasoning
-Microwave for 1-2 Minutes, til cheese is melted
-Serve with Bread, Chips, or Bread Sticks

Sweet Potato Chips

Ingredients

-1 Large Sweet Potato
-1-2 tbsp Olive Oil
-½ tsp salt

Directions

-Wash and Peal Sweet Potato

– Cut Potato into 1/8 In Thick slices
-Toss with Olive Oil and Salt
– Place Sweet Potatoes in single layer on plate
-Microwave on Medium for 1 ½ Minutes
-Turn over Microwave 1 ½ Minutes
-Cook for 30 seconds til Potato slices are crisp

Panko & Parmesan Topped Zucchini

Ingredients

-2 Zucchini's cut into ½ inch slices
-1/2 cup Panko Breadcrumbs
-1 tbsp grated Parmesan Cheese

-1/2 tsp Garlic Powder
-1/2 tsp Onion Powder
-1/4 tsp salt
-1/4 tsp black pepper
-1 tbsp mayonnaise

Directions

-Microwave Zucchini Slices for 15-30 seconds
-Mix Panko Bread Crumbs, Parmesan Cheese, Garlic Powder, Onion Powder, Salt, & Pepper
-Add small amount of Mayonnaise to zucchini and spoon on mix.
-Press Down Lightly
-Broil on 350 til breadcrumbs are brown

Microwave Nachos

Ingredients
-Tortillas
-1/2 Cup Cooked Seasoned Ground Beef
-1/2 – ¾ Cup Shredded Cheddar Cheese
-Sliced Green Onion
-Jalapeno Slices
-1/2 Avocado
-Sour Cream
-Salsa

Directions
-Arrange Chips as single layer
-Add Ground Beef to each chip
-Top with generous amount of cheese
-Add 1 Slice of Jalapeno to each chip
-Sprinkle on Green Onion
-Microwave for 1-2 Minutes Until Cheese is melted
-Top Each chip with avocado, Sour Cream & Salsa

Spinach Dip

Ingredients
-2 Cups Frozen Spinach
-8 Oz Low Fat Cream Cheese
-2 tbsp Greek Yogurt
-3/4 Cup Shredded Cheddar Cheese
-1/4 Cup Shredded Parmesan Cheese
-1/4 tsp Garlic Powder
-1/2 tsp salt

Directions

-Thaw and Strain Spinach
-Mix Cream Cheese, Yogurt,
-Stir In Cheddar, Parmesan, Garlic Powder, & salt
-Stir In Spinach
-Heat in Microwave for 30 seconds, stir and repeat til heated throughout
-Serve with sour dough bread cubes, chips, or veggies

Spicy Queso Dip

Ingredients
-1 LB Sausage
-32 Oz Cheese Dip
-15 Oz Black Beans
-10 Oz Tomatoes

Directions
-Cook Sausage, til crumbly. Drain fat

-Microwave Cheese Dip
-Stir in Black Beans
-Stir In Sausage
-Stir In Tomato
-Microwave 60 seconds.
-Serve with Tortilla Chips

Cheesy Bean Dip

Ingredients
-16 Oz Can Refried Beans
-16 oz Salsa
-3 Cup Shredded Cheddar Cheese
-1 Can Jalapeno Cheddar Cheese Dip

Directions

-Place all Ingredients in a Microwave Safe Dish
-Mix Well
-Cover with plastic wrap
-Cook on HIGH until cheese is melted.
-Stir Every Minute

Soups & Sandwiches

A warm soup on a cold day makes the world of difference in what comfort food is meant to be. Sandwiches take a twist of flavor on something that is considered simple. Enjoy not only what these dishes have to offer but allow yourself to expand on the flavors making your own meals in the future.

Page Number

35. Black Bean Soup
36. Chicken & Rice Soup
37. Homemade Chicken Noodle Soup
38. Cabbage Soup
39. Minestrone
40. Potato Soup
41. Baked Ham Sandwich
42. Classic Monte Cristo
43. Grilled Macaroni & Cheese Sandwich

44. Meatball Sandwich
45. Open Face Hot Roast Beef Sandwich
46. Pineapple Pulled Pork Sandwich

Black Bean Soup

Ingredients

-¾ Cup Canned Black Beans, Rinsed & Drained
-3/4 Cup Chicken Broth
-1/3 Cup Salsa
-1/4 Cup Whole Kernel Corn
-Dash of Hot Sauce
-1 tsp Lime Juice
-1/2 Cup Shredded Cheddar Cheese

-1 tbsp Chopped Green Onion

Directions

-Combine Black Beans, Chicken Broth, Salsa, Corn, & hot Sauce
-Cover & Microwave on HIGH for 2 minutes, Til Hot
-Serve with Drizzle of Lime Juice
-Sprinkle with cheese and Green Onion

Chicken & Rice Soup

Ingredients

-2 tbsp Uncooked Instant Rice
-1 1/2 tsp reduced sodium chicken bouillon
-1 tsp dried celery flakes
-1 tsp dried parsley
-1/4 tsp dried minced onion
-1/8 tsp pepper
-3/4 Cup Boiling Water

-1 Can Chunk White, Chicken, Drained

Directions

- Combine Rice, Bouillon Cube, Celery Flakes, Parsley, Onion, & Pepper
-Pour Boiling Water over Ingredients, Cover Let Stand for 5 minutes
-Stir In Chicken
-Microwave on HIGH uncovered for 1-2 Minutes

Homemade Chicken Noodle Soup

Ingredients
-1 Cup Chicken Broth
-1/2 Cup Shredded Rotisserie Chicken
-1/4 Cup Thinly Sliced Carrots
-1/4 Cup Egg Noodle
-1 tbsp Sliced Scallions
-1 tsp Fresh Lemon Juice

-1/8 tsp Kosher Salt
-1/8 tsp Black Pepper

Directions
-Microwave Noodles til tender, Strain
-Combine Chicken Broth, Chicken, Carrot, Noodles, Carrots, Scallion, Lemon Juice, Salt & Pepper.
-Cover & Microwave until Carrots are tender around 7 minutes

Cabbage Soup

Ingredients

- 1 Cup Green Cabbage, Chopped or Shredded
-2 tsp Butter
-1/2 Chopped Onion
-1/4 Cup Chopped Scallions
-1/2 tsp Salt
-1/2 tsp Black Pepper
-1/4 tsp Sugar
-4 oz Chicken Broth

-1/4 Cup Skim Milk
-1/4 Cup Shredded Carrots

Directions

-Heat Butter 40 seconds til melted.
-Add Cabbage, Scallions, Salt, Pepper, & Sugar. Cook on HIGH 4-6 Min
-Add Broth, Cook on HIGH 15 Minutes
-Add Warm Milk
-Stir in Carrots
-Season to Taste

Minestrone

Ingredients

- 1 Cup Sliced Carrot, Celery, & Zucchini
-1/2 Cup Diced Yellow Pepper
-1 Small Onion Chopped
-1 tbsp Olive Oil
-1 Can Cannellini Beans
-1 Can Beef Broth
-1 Can Diced Tomatoes
-1 Cup Medium Pasta Shells
-1/2 tsp Dried Basil

-1/2 tsp Salt & Pepper

Directions

-Combine Carrots, Celery, Zucchini, Yellow Pepper & Onion.
-Toss with Oil
-Microwave on HIGH for 3 Minutes
-Stir in Remaining Ingredients.
-Cover & Cook on HIGH for 9-11 Minutes

Potato Soup

Ingredients

-3/4 Cup Water
-3 tbsp Cubed Potatoes
-1 tbsp White Onion, Chopped
-2 tbsp Cheddar Cheese
-1 tbsp Cooked Bacon
-2 tsp Cornstarch
-1/2 Cup Chicken Stock
-1/2 Cup Milk
-Salt & Pepper to Taste

-Sour Cream for Garnish

Directions

- Microwave Potatoes & Water for 3-4 Minutes, til Tender
-Drain Water
-Stir In Cooked Bacon, Cheese, Onion, & Cornstarch
-Stir In Stock & Milk
-Salt & Pepper to Taste
-Microwave for 2 1/2 - 3 Minutes. Stir Occasionally
- Serve with Sour Cream

Baked Ham Sandwich

Ingredients

-1-2 Hawaiian Sweet Roll
-2-6 Slices Honey Ham
-1 Slice Muenster Cheese
-Pat of Butter
-Honey Mustard

Directions

-Slice open Sweet Roll
-Add Ham & Cheese to Bottom Slice
-Add Top Piece of Sweet Roll
-Pat Top of Slice with Butter
-Microwave 1 Minute, Til Cheese Is Melted
-Flip Over Sandwich
-Open Sandwich, Add Mustard To Bottom Roll

Monte Cristo

Ingredients

-2 Large Eggs
-1/4 Cup Milk
-1/4 tsp Sald
-1/8 tsp Pepper
-1 tbsp Dijon Mustard
-4 Slices Texas Toast
-4 Slices Swiss Cheese
-4 Slices Roast Turkey
-2 Slices Baked Ham
-6 tbsp Red Raspberry Jam
-2 tbsp Butter
-2 tsp Powdered Sugar (Optional)

Direction

-Beat Eggs, Milk, Salt & Pepper
-Spread Mustard on 2 Slices of Toast
-Top Each Slice with 1 Slice of Cheese, 2 Slices Turkey, 1 Slice Ham
-Add Remaining Cheese

-Spread 1 tbsp Jam on 2 remaining Slices of Toast, Close Sandwich
-Melt 1 tbsp Butter in Non Stick Pan
-Place Sandwich in Egg Mixture for 10 Seconds. Flip and Soak
-Place Sandwich in Hot Pan
-Reduce heat to Medium-Low. Cook 6-7 Minutes til Golden Brown
-Melt Remaining Butter
-Flip Sandwich & toast 4-5 Minutes til Golden Brown
-Optional Microwave remaining Jam for 45 Seconds, Whisk Into Syrup. Sprinkle Powdered Sugar over Sandwich.
-Serve with Melted Jam

Grilled Macaroni & Cheese Sandwich

Ingredients

-4 Slices Bread
-2 tbsp Butter
-4 Slices Cheddar Cheese
- 1 Serving Macaroni & Cheese

Directions

-Make Macaroni & Cheese (follow Directions on Box)
-Spread 1/2 tbsp Butter on 1 side of each slice of Bread
-Place Cheese on Top of each Un-Buttered side of Bread
-Spread 1/2 Macaroni & Cheese Evenly on Each Slice of Bread
-Place Both Sandwiches Butter side down in medium hot pan
- Cook Til Bread is Golden Brown. Flip & Repeat

Meatball Sandwich

Ingredients

-2 Slices Provolone Cheese
-3 Oz Frozen Meatballs
-7 oz Spaghetti Sauce
-1 Hoagie Roll

Directions

-Microwave Meatballs according to Packaging
- Add Spaghetti Sauce. Return To Microwave. Heat Til Bubbling
- Spoon Meatballs onto Hoagie, Add Desired Sauce
-Place 2 Slices of Provolone over Hoagie.
- Place Back in Microwave til Cheese is Melted

Open Face Hot Roast Beef Sandwich

Ingredients

-6-8 Oz Sliced Beef
-1 Slices White Bread
- 1/4 Cup Peas
-1 Potato
-1 Jar Gravy
1/8 Cup Milk
-1 tbsp Butter
-Dash Salt & Pepper

Direction

- Peel Potato, Cut into Cubes. Microwave for 5 minutes, Stir, Microwave til

Tender
-Place Pea in Microwave for 5 Minutes
-Add Butter, Milk, Salt & Pepper to Potatoes & Mash til Smooth
-Tear Up Beef and spread over bread
-Strain Peas
-Microwave Bread & Beef for 30 Seconds.
- Stir Peas into Potatoes, Pour Over Beef
-Heat Jar of Gravy per Directions
-Pour desired amount over entire dish

Pineapple Pulled Pork Sandwich

Ingredients

-Cooking Spray
-3 Pounds Pork Shoulder
-Salt & Pepper
-12 Oz Pineapple Flavored Topping
-3/4 Cup BBQ Sauce
-12 Kaiser Rolls or/
-24 Hawaiian Sweet Rolls

Directions

-Heat Oven to 350 F. Spray Pan with Oil.
-Season Pork with Salt & Pepper.
-Cover Pan with Foil.

-Slow Roast for 4 Hours until Meat falls Apart
-Collect 1/2 Cup of Pan Dripping, Pineapple Topping,& BBQ Sauce
-Whisk Well, Microwave for 45 Seconds
-Stir In Shredded Pork. Microwave 45 Seconds
-Serve Pork Over Kaiser Roll or Hawaiian Roll

Beef, Pork & Lamb

Beef, Pork & Lamb can be cooked in the Microwave. It may be taboo, something you will never do but I would do this book a disservice to not include these.

Page Number

48. Meat Loaf
49. Meat Balls
50. Beef & Cheese Enchiladas
51. Ground Beef Tacos
52. Sirloin Steak
53. BBQ Pork Chop
54. Pork Tenderloin
55. Lamb Chop

Meat Loaf

Ingredients

- 1 Large Egg
-5 tbsp Ketchup
2 tbsp Mustard
-1/2 Cup Dried Bread Crumbs
-2 tbsp Onion Soup Mix
-1/4 tsp Salt
1/4 tsp Black Pepper
-1 LB Ground Beef
-1/4 Cup Sugar
-2 tbsp Brown Sugar
-2 tbsp Cider Vinegar

Directions

- Combine Egg, 2 tbsp Ketchup, Mustard, Bread Crumbs, Soup Mix, Salt, & Pepper. Mix Beef in Thoroughly with hand. Shape into a Loaf
-Place Loaf in Shallow Microwave Safe Dish, Cover & Cook on HIGH for 10-12 Minutes. Continue Cooking til their is no pink remaining.
-Combine Sugar, Remaining Ketchup, & Vinegar.
-Drizzle over Meat Loaf. Cover & Microwave on HIGH 2-3 Minute.
-Let Stand 10 minutes before serving

Meatballs

Ingredients

-2 LBs Frozen Fully Cooked Meatballs
- 2 Medium Carrots, Julienne
- 1 Small Onion, Sliced
-1 Small Greed Pepper, Julienne
-1 Garlic Clove, Minced
-1 Jar Sweet & Sour Sauce
-4 1/2 tsp soy sauce
-Microwave Rice

Directions

-Microwave Meatballs with Carrots, Onion, Pepper, & Garlic.
-Mix Sweet & Sour Sauce with Soy Sauce and Pour over Meatballs
-Microwave covered on HIGH 6-8 Minutes. Stir Occasionally
-Serve with Rice

Beef & Cheese Enchiladas

Ingredients

-1/2 LB Ground Beef
-2 tbsp Chopped Onion
-2 Cups Shredded Cheese
-1 Can Enchilada Sauce
-1 tbsp Canned Chopped Green Chilies
-6 Corn Tortilla
-Shredded Lettuce & Sour Cream (Optional)

Directions

Crumble Beef & Onion in dish. Cover & cook on HIGH 2-3 Minutes
-Drain Once Beef shows no Pink.
-Stir In 1 Cup of Cheese, 1/4 Cup Enchilada Sauce & Chilies
- Place 1/2 Cup Beef Mixture in each tortilla. Roll and Place in Grease Pan

-Top with Remaining Enchilada Sauce
-Microwave on High 5-6 Minutes.
-Sprinkle with remaining Cheese
-Microwave til cheese is melted
-Serve with Lettuce, Sour Cream & Hot Sauce

Ground Beef Tacos

Ingredients

-1LB Ground Beef
-1 1/2 tsp Chili Powder
-1/2 tsp salt
-1/2 tsp Garlic Powder
-1/8 Cayenne Pepper
-1/4 Cup Water
-8 Taco Shells
-2 Cups Shredded Mexican Cheese
-2 Cups Shredded Lettuce
-1/4 Cup Finely Chopped Onion
-1 Medium Tomato, Chopped

-Optional Hot Sauce, Sour Cream, Guacamole

Directions

-Crumble Ground Beef, Cover. Microwave for 5 Minutes
-Drain, then Stir in Chili Powder, Salt, Garlic, Cayenne Pepper & Water
-Cover & Microwave for 3-4 Minutes. Til No Pink
-Fill Each Taco Shell with Beef.
-Top With Cheese, Lettuce, Tomato
-Optional Hot Sauce, Sour Cream, & Guacamole

Sirloin Steak

Ingredients

-1 Sirloin Steal
-Salt & Pepper to Taste or
-Pat of Butter

Directions

- Let Steak reach room temperature

-Pat Down any moisture with Paper Towel
-Season with Salt & Pepper
-Microwave for 3-4 minutes on HIGH
-Flip Steak Over Cook Additional 2-3 Minutes
-Pat of Butter Before Serving
*Cooking Time Varies on Thickness

BBQ Pork Chops

Ingredients

-6 Boneless Pork Loin Chops
-1 Medium Onion, Chopped
-1 Cup Ketchup
-1/2 Cup Water
-1/2 Cup Chopped Celery
-2 tbsp Lemon Juice
-1 tbsp Brown Sugar
-1 tbsp Worchestershire Sauce
-1/2 tsp Salt
-1/2 tsp Ground Mustard
-BBQ Sauce
- 1 tsp Cornstarch
-1 tbsp Cold Water

Directions

- Place Pork Chops in Microwave Safe Dish
-Mix Onion, Ketchup, Water, Celery, Lemon Juice, Brown Sugar, Worchestershire, Salt, & Ground Mustard.
-Pour Mixture over Pork Chops
-Cover with Plastic Wrap, Leave 1 side uncovered to vent

-Microwave on HIGH 11-13 minutes, til juice runs clear
-Keep Warm Til Ready To Serve
-Combine Cornstarch & Cold Water. Mix til Smooth
-Add Mixture to BBQ. Stir Well.
-Microwave 30-45 Seconds
Serve as side dipping sauce

Pork Tenderloin

Ingredients

-Pork Tenderloin
-1/2 tbsp Onion Powder
-1/2 tbsp Garlic Powder
-2 tsp Black Pepper
-1 tsp Salt
-3 Cups Carrots
-1 tbsp Olive Oil

Directions

-Trim Fat From Tenderloin
-Sprinkle Onion Powder, Garlic Powder, 1 tsp Black Pepper over Pork
-Drizzle Olive Oil & Rub Seasoning thoroughly over Pork
-Place In Microwave Safe Dish

-Chop Carrots & Toss in Olive Oil, Salt & Pepper
-Add Carrots to Dish
-Microwave 10 Minutes. Flip Pork & Mix Carrots
-Microwave Additional 10 Minutes
-Cook Until No Pink and Clear Juices

Lamb Chop

Ingredients

-4 Lamb Chops / Chump Chop
-2 tbsp Fruit Chutney
-1 tsp Curry Powder
-1 tbsp Brown Sugar
-2 tsp Soy Sauce
-1 tsp Vinegar

Directions

-Trim Fat From Chops
-Combine Fruit Chutney, Curry Powder, Brown Sugar, Soy Sauce & Vinegar
-Pour Over Lamb.
-Cook 5 Minutes on HIGH til Cooked Through & Tender

Chicken, Turkey, Hen & Duck

Just like with Beef, Poultry is a Microwavable meal. Below are a few of the examples of the different flavors you can incorporate into your dishes, using a Microwave

Page Number

57. Chipotle Ranch Chicken Tacos
58. Honey Lemon Chicken Enchiladas
59. Italian Chicken Cordon Bleu
60. Chicken Fajitas
61. Chicken Kiev
62. Parmesan Chicken
63. Stuffed Turkey Breast
64. Turkey Enchiladas
65. Cornish Hen
66. Zapped Duck

Chipotle Ranch Chicken Tacos

Ingredients

-2 Cups Shredded Rotisserie Chicken
-2 Cups Frozen Corn, thawed
- 1/4 Cup Pico De Gallo
-8 Taco Shells or Corn Tortillas
- 1 Cup Shredded Cheese
-1 Cup Coleslaw
-6 Radishes, Thinly Sliced
-1/2 Cup Chipotle Ranch Salad Dressing
- 3 Jalapeno Peppers, Thinly Sliced

Directions

-Combine Chicken, Corn, Pico De Gallo in Glass Bowl
-Microwave on HIGH 1-2 minutes
-Spoon Chicken into Taco Shells/ Tortillas
- Top with Coleslaw, Radish, Jalapeno, & Cheese

-Drizzle Chipotle Ranch over Entire Taco

Honey Lemon Chicken Enchiladas

Ingredients

-1/4 Cup Honey
-2 tbsp Lemon or Lime Juice
-1 tbsp Canola Oil
-2 tsp Chili Powder
-1/4 tsp Garlic Powder
-3 Cups Shredded Cooked Chicken
-2 Cans Green Enchilada Sauce
- 12 Corn Tortillas
-3/4 Cups Shredded Cheddar Cheese
-1 Medium Sliced Green Onion
- 2 Chopped Tomato

Directions

-Combine Honey, Lemon/Lime Juice, Canola Oil, Chili Powder, & Garlic Powder
-Add Shredded Chicken & Toss to Coat
-Pour Enchilada Sauce Into a Greased Dish Pan
-Place 1/4 Cup Chicken Mixture Into A Tortilla
-Roll & Place In Pan

-Top Entire Tray With 1 Can Enchilada Sauce
-Microwave Covered on HIGH 11-13 Minutes
-Sprinkle on Cheese, Onion & Tomato

Italian Chicken Cordon Bleu

Ingredients

-2 tbsp Butter, Cubed
-1/2 tsp Rubbed Sage
-6 Boneless Skinless Chicken Breast Halves
-1 Medium Green Pepper, Sliced
-1/3 Cup Sliced Mushroom
- 1 Can Tomato Sauce
-1 tsp Sugar
-1 tsp Dried Oregano
-1/2 tsp salt
-1/2 tsp Garlic Powder
- 1/2 tsp Lemon Pepper Seasoning
-6 Slices Deli Ham
-6 Slices Swiss Cheese
-Minute Rice

Directions

-Mix Butter & Sage in Microwave safe Dish
-Microwave for 30 Seconds til Butter Melts
-Coat Chicken in Melted Butter
-Top With Bell Pepper & Mushroom.
-Cook on HIGH for 8-10 Minute, Flip Twice
- Remove Chicken When Juices Run Clear
-Add Tomato Sauce, Sugar, Oregano, Salt, Garlic Powder & Lemon Pepper
-Cook Sauce for 2 minutes.
-Return Chicken to the Pan.
-Top with Ham, Cheese, Green Pepper & Mushroom.
-Cook 2 minutes til Cheese Melts
-Serve Chicken Over Rice

Chicken Fajita

Ingredients

- Chicken Breast
- 1/2 Medium Onion
- 1 Red Pepper
- 1 Green Pepper
- Fajita Seasoning Packet
- 2 Tortilla
- Sour Cream, Salsa, Guacamole Optional

Directions

- Slice Green & Red Pepper
- Slice 1/2 an Onion add
- Add To Bowl
- Sprinkle 1/2 Fajita Packet into Bowl. Toss
- Slice Chicken Breast Into Strips
- Add Remaining Fajita Mix to Bowl. Toss Everything
- Cover Bowl & Microwave on HIGH 5 Minute
- Stir & Microwave on HIGH 5 Minutes
- Cook in 1 Minute Intervals til Fully Cooked
- Serve with Warm Tortilla
- Optional Salsa, Sour Cream, Guacamole

Chicken Kiev

Ingredients

- 5 tbsp Butter
- 1/2 tsp Chives, Minced
- 1/4 tsp Garlic Powder
- 1/4 tsp White Pepper
- 4 Boneless Skinless Chicken Breast Halves
- 1/3 Cup Corn flake, Crumbles
- 1 tbsp Grated Parmesan Cheese
- 1/2 tsp Dried Parsley
- 1/4 tsp Paprika

Directions

- Combine 3 tbsp Butter, Chives, Garlic Powder, & pepper.
- Shape into 4 cubes. Cover & Freeze
- Flatten Chicken Breast to 1/4 in Thickness
- Add Butter Cube in Center of each Chicken
- Fold Long sides of Chicken over Butter. Secure with Toothpick
- In Bowl Combine Corn Flakes, Cheese, Parsley & Paprika
- Melt Remaining Butter.
- Dip Chicken In Butter; Coat in Corn Flake Mixture
- Place Seam Side Down in Microwave Safe Pan
- Cook Uncovered on HIGH 5-6 Minutes
- Continue Cooking In 1 Minute Intervals Til Chicken Juices Run Clear

Parmesan Chicken

Ingredients

- 2 Boneless Skinless Chicken Breast
- 4 tsp Soy Sauce
- 1/4 tsp Garlic Powder
- 1/8 tsp Black Pepper
- 1/ 4 Cup Grated Parmesan Cheese
- 1 tsp Butter

Directions

- Place Chicken in Dish
- Mix In Bowl Soy Sauce, Garlic Powder, Pepper
- Pour Mixture over Chicken
- Sprinkle Chicken With Parmesan Cheese
- Place Small Amount of Butter on Chicken
- Cook on HIGH for 4-5 Minutes. Til Juices Run Clear

Stuffed Turkey Breast

Ingredients

-1 Box Herb Stuffing
-1/2 Cup Dried Cranberries
-1 Can Chicken Broth
-8 Turkey Breast Cutlets
-2 Jars Turkey Gravy

Directions

Coat Microwave Safe Baking Dish with Cooking Spray
-Combine Stuffing, Dried Cranberries & Broth
-Mix Well
- Place Stuffing Mixture equally between centers of Turkey Cutlets
-Roll Up Cutlets & Place in Pan
-Pour Gravy over the Cutlets.
-Microwave for 14-18 minutes til their is no pink remaining.

Turkey Enchilada

Ingredients

-1 LB Lean Ground Turkey
-2 Cans Tomato Sauce
--3 tsp dried Minced Onion
-1/2 tsp Garlic Powder
-1/2 tsp Black Pepper
-1.4 tsp Salt
-4 Tortillas
-2/3 Cups Shredded Cheddar Cheese

Directions

-Crumble Ground Turkey & Microwave til Brown.
-Stir In Onion, Garlic, Pepper & Salt.
-In Round Microwave Safe Bowl Coat with Cooking Spray
-Layer 1 Tortilla, 3/4 Cup Meat Mixture, & Handful of Cheese
-Repeat Layering 3 more times
-Cover Dish & Microwave until Cheese is Melted 4-5 Minutes
-Let Stand 5 Minutes
-Cut & Serve

Cornish Hen

Ingredients

-1 Cup Chopped Mushroom
-2 tbsp Butter
-1 Cup Bulgur
-1 3/4 Cup Chicken Broth
-1 tsp Salt
-1/8 tsp Black Pepper
-1/3 Cup Chopped Pecans
-2 Cornish Hens
-3 tbsp Liquid Gravy Mix
-3 tbsp Water

Directions

- Combine Mushroom, Butter, Bulgar & Broth in Casserole Dish
-Cover and Microwave on HIGH 4-6 Minutes
-Stir Lightly, Recover Cook on Medium 9-10 Minutes
-Let Stand 5 Minutes when most liquid is absorbed
-Mix In Salt, Pepper & Pecans
-Loosely Stuff Hen with 1/3 mixture
-Skewer Opening Shut
- Arrange Hens Breast Up in Microwave
-Brush Each Hen with Gravy Glaze
-Microwave on HIGH 6-8 Minutes per Pound
-Cook Additional Minute Til Hen Juice Runs Clear
-Brush Hen with Browning Glaze. Let Stand 5 Minutes

Zapped Duck

Ingredients

-1 5LB Whole Duck
-1/4 Cup Red Wine Vinegar
-3 tbsp Sugar
-1 Cup Duck Giblet Stock
-2 tbsp Sherry

Directions

-Place Duck Breast Side Down.
-Microwave on HIGH 15 Minutes
-Pour off Fat. Turn Duck Breast Side Up
-Microwave on HIGH 15 Minutes
-After Duck Has Cooked. Pour off Fat.
Place Duck Breast Side Down in Oven
-500 F 10 Minutes, Turn Duck Over
-Cook 5 Minutes
Let Stand 5-15 Minutes, Covered In Foil

Sherry Duck Sauce

-Combine Vinegar & Sugar. Microwave on HIGH 3 Minutes
-Stir, Microwave on HIGH 1-2 Minutes til it Begins to Brown & Thicken
-Stir Duck Dripping into Mix. Microwave on High 2 Min til Boiling.
-Add Sherry. Mix
-Microwave on HIGH 5 Minutes or Until Boiling

Fish & Seafood

Page Number

68. Cod Delight
69. Poached Salmon & Cucumber Sauce
70. Salmon w/ Tarragon Sauce

Cod Delight

Ingredients

- 1 Small Tomato
- 1/3 Cup Finely Chopped Onion
- 2 tbsp Water
- 2 tbsp Canola Oil
- 4-5 tsp Lemon Juice
- 1 tsp Dried Parsley
- 1/2 tsp Dried Basil
- 1 Garlic Clove, Minced
- 1/8 tsp Salt
- 4 Cod Fillets
- 1tsp Seafood Seasoning

Directions

- Combine Tomato, Onion, Water, Canola Oil, Lemon Juice, Parsley, Basil, Garlic, & Salt.
- Place Cod in Baking Dish. Top with Mixture.
- Sprinkle with Seafood Seasoning
- Microwave, Covered on HIGH 5-6 Minutes, til Cod Begins to Flake

Poached Salmon & Cucumber Sauce

Ingredients
-1 Cup Water
-1/2 Cup Dry White Wine
-1 Small Onion, Sliced
-2 Springs Fresh Parsley
-1/4 tsp Salt
-5 Peppercorns
-4 Salmon Steaks
-1/2 Cup Sour Cream
-1/3 Cup Chopped Cucumber
-1 tbsp Finely Chopped Onion
-1/4 tsp Salt
-1/4 tsp Dried Basil

Directions

-Coat Pan in Cooking Spray
-Combine Water, Wine, Onion, Parsley, & Salt

-Microwave on HIGH until Boiling 2-3 Minutes
-Add Salmon Steaks to Dish
-Cover & Microwave until Fish Flakes 5-6 Minutes
-Combine Sour Cream, Cucumber, 1 tbsp Chopped Onion, 1/4 tsp salt, & 1/4 tsp Basil
-Serve Poached Salmon with Cucumber Sauce

Salmon W/ Tarragon Sauce

Ingredients

-4 Salmon Fillets
-1/4 tsp salt
-1/4 tsp White Pepper
-2 tbsp White Wine
-1 tbsp Butter
-1 Green Onion Finely Chopped
-1 tbsp All Purpose Flour

-1 tsp Dijon Mustard
-1/2 tsp Dried Tarragon
-2/3 Cup 2% Milk

Directions

-Place Salmon in Oil Sprayed Dish.
-Sprinkle Salmon with Salt & Pepper.
-Pour Wine over top
-Cover & Microwave on HIGH 4-6 Minutes
-Remove Salmon from Dish
-Add Butter & Onion to juices.
-Microwave on HIGH for 1 Minute
-Stir in Flour, Mustard & Tarragon til Blended
-Gradually Stir In Milk
-Cook Uncovered 1-2 Minutes, Until thick. Stir Every 30 Seconds
-Serve Sauce with Salmon

Sides

No Dish is Complete Without Sides, that are able to complete A Meal. As Im sure you have guessed by now you can microwave a plethora of meals in the microwave. So below are not the simple microwaved vegetable that you can add to your dish. Below are simple sides that can be customized by you to fit your main dish.

Page Number

72. Baked Potato
73. Coconut Acorn Squash
74. Egg Fried Rice
75. Steamed Rice
76. Single Serve Macaroni & Cheese
77. Loaded Cauliflower
78. Green Bean Casserole

79. Broccoli Casserole
80. Southern Corn Salad

Baked Potato

Ingredients

-1 Potato
-Dash of Salt
-Dash of Pepper
-Pat of Butter

Directions

-Wash Potato thoroughly
-Pat Dry
-Pierce 3-4 times with a Fork
-Place in Microwave for 4 Minutes
-Flip Over & Microwave 3 Minutes
-If not tender Continue Microwaving in 1 Minute Increments
-Let Rest 2 Minutes
-Split Potato Open, season with Salt, Pepper, & Butter

Coconut Acorn Squash

Ingredients

-2 Small Acorn Squash
-1/4 Cup Mango Chutney
-1/4 Cup Shredded Coconut
-3 tbsp Butter
-1/4 tsp Salt
-1/8 tsp Black Pepper

Directions

-Cut Squash in 1/2 Lengthwise. Remove Seeds
-Place on Dish, Cut side Down
-Microwave, Covered on HIGH 10-12 minutes
-Mix Mango Chutney, Coconut, & Melted Butter in Bowl.
-Flip Squash Over. Spoon Chutney Mix in Center of Squash
-Sprinkle on Salt & Pepper
-Microwave, Covered on HIGH for 2-3 Minutes

Egg Fried Rice

Ingredients

-1 Cup Minute Rice
-2 tbsp Frozen Peas
-2 tbsp Red Pepper, Chopped
-1/2 stalk of Green Onion, Sliced
- Small Pinch of Mung Bean (Optional)
-1 Large Egg
-1 tbsp Soy Sauce
-1/2 tsp Sesame Oil (Optional)
-1/2 tsp Onion Powder
-1/4 tsp Five Spice Powder

Directions

-Microwave Minute Rice in Bowl
-Place Peas, Red Pepper, Onion, & Mung Bean on Top
-Cook for 1 Minute 15 Seconds
-Beat Egg, Mix in Soy Sauce, Sesame Oil, Onion Powder, & Five Spice
-Pour Egg Mix over Rice. Mix Thoroughly
-Cover Bowl with Cling Film. Puncture 3 Small Holes in Film
-Microwave 1 Minute 15 Seconds
-Stir Mixture
-Let Stand 1 Minute

Rice

Ingredients

-1 1/2 Cups Jasmine, Basmati, or White Rice
-2 1/4 Cup Water

Directions

-Measure Rice into Microwave Safe Container
- Pour Water Into Bowl
-Stir Rice & Pour Water Out

-Repeat til Water is Barley Cloudy
-Add Enough Water to Cover Rice buy 1 In
-Microwave on HIGH for 9 Minutes
-Rest for 3 Minutes
-Fluff with Fork

Single Serve Macaroni & Cheese

Ingredients

-1/3 Cup Elbow Noodles
-1/2 Cup Water
-1/4 Cup Milk
-1/2 Cup Shredded Cheese

Directions

-Measure Noodles & Water In A Bowl
-Microwave on HIGH for 2 Minutes, Stir
-Microwave 1 Minute. Stir
-Microwave 1 More Minute, Stir
-Microwave til All Water Is Absorbed

-Stir In Milk, and Cheese.
-Microwave 30-60 Seconds
-Stir Well

Loaded Cauliflower

Ingredients

-1 LB Cauliflower
-4 oz Sour Cream
-1 Cup Shredded Cheddar Cheese
-2 Slices Cooked Bacon
-2 tbsp Chives
-3 tbsp Butter
-1/4 tsp Garlic Powder
-Salt & Pepper to Taste

Directions

-Cut Cauliflower Into Florets
-Add 2 tbsp Water. Microwave 5-6 Minutes
- Cook til Tender. Drain Excess Water
-Dice Florets, or Use Food Processor.

Mix In Butter, Garlic Powder, Sour Cream, Chives
- Add 1/2 of Cheese & Mix
-Season with Salt & Pepper
-Top Cauliflower with Cheese & Bacon
-Microwave Til Cheese Is Melted

Green Bean Casserole

Ingredients

- 1 Can Cream of Mushroom Soup
-1/2 Cup Milk
-3 Cans Cut Green Beans. Drained
-1/4 tsp Black Pepper
-1 1/2 Cup Fried Onion

Directions

-Mix together Cream of Mushroom Soup & Milk
-Add In Green Beans, Pepper & 1 Cup Fried Onion
-Transfer to Microwave Safe Dish
-Microwave on HIGH 4 Minutes
-Gently Stir Casserole. Top with Remaining Onions
-Microwave on HIGH til Heated Through 3 Minutes

Broccoli Casserole

Ingredients

-6 Cups Broccoli Florets
-1/2 Yellow Onion Diced
-4 tbsp Butter, Melted
-10 3/4 Oz Cream of Mushroom Soup
-3/4 Cup Mayonnaise
-2 Large Eggs
-1/2 tsp Salt
-1/4 tsp Black Pepper
-2 Cups Shredded Cheddar Cheese

Directions

-Microwave Broccoli til Tender. 5 Minutes
-Dice Broccoli
-Mix Broccoli, Butter, Soup, Mayonnaise, Eggs, Salt, Pepper, & 1 Cup Cheese
-Pour Into Microwave Safe Dish

-Microwave 3 Minutes. Til Fully Cooked
- Pour Remaining Cheese over Top
-Microwave Til Cheese Is Melted

Corn Salad

Ingredients

-5 Ears of Fresh Corn
-1 Small Red Onion, Minced
-3 tbsp Cider Vinegar
-3 tbsp Olive Oil
-1/2 tsp Salt
-1/2 tsp Black Pepper
-1/2 Cup Fresh Basil, Chopped

Directions

-Slice the Stem of the Ear of Corn Off
-Microwave 2 At A Time on HIGH 3 Minutes
-Let Corn Cool. Squeeze Corn At Top
-Let Corn Slip out of Husk
-Cut Kernels of Cob
-Combine Kernels With Vinegar, Olive Oil, Onion, Salt, & Pepper

-Before Serving Add Basil & Stir

Sauces

Below are a few of the Sauces that are able to be made in the Microwave. These Sauces are very simple and can be improved on with your personal tastes and creativity.

Page Number

82. Easy White Sauce
83. Tomato Sauce
84. Hollandaise

Easy White Sauce

Ingredients

-1 Cup Milk
-2 tbsp Flour
-1 tbsp Butter
-1/4 tsp Salt
Cheese Sauce: 1/2 to 3/4 Cup Grated Cheddar Cheese
Curry Sauce: 1-2 tsp Curry Powder
Horseradish Sauce: 1 tsp Horseradish
Mustard Sauce: 2 tbsp Prepared Mustard, 1 Dash Worcestershire

Directions

-Combine Melted Butter, Flour & Salt in Bowl
-Gradually Add Milk
-Stir Til Smooth
-Cook on MEDIUM Heat for 6-7 Minutes. Stir Occasionally

Cheese Sauce
-Stir In 1/2 to 3/4 Cup Cheese
-Microwave High 1-2 Minutes Til Melted

Curry Sauce
-Stir in 1 to 2 tsp Curry Powder

Horseradish Sauce
-Stir In Horseradish

Mustard Sauce
-Stir in 2 tbsp Prepared Mustard & Dash of Worcestershire Sauce

Tomato Sauce

Instructions

-2 28Oz Cans Whole Peeled Tomatoes
-Salt & Pepper
-Optional Garlic, Basil, Oregano, Thyme

Directions

-Pour Tomatoes into Strainer. Collect Liquid in Bowl
-Crush Tomatoes with hand releasing Juices
-Microwave Juice on HIGH til liquid is thick like Ketchup 20-25 Minutes
- Add Crushed Tomatoes Back into Sauce.
-Cool to Room Temperature
-Add Salt & Pepper to Taste
-Optional Additions
(Oregano, Basil, Garlic, Thyme)

Hollandaise Sauce

Ingredients

- 2 Egg Yolks
- 1/4 Lemon Juice
- 1 Pinch Salt
- 1 Pinch Cayenne Pepper
- 1/4 Cup Melted Butter

Directions

-Beat Egg Yolk, Lemon Juice, alt, Cayenne Pepper, together til Smooth
-Slowly Add In Melted Butter, Stirring Continuously
-Heat in Microwave 15-20 Seconds. Whisk

Desserts

Desserts are for some the most favorite part of the meal. For others it is a delicious treat that can be eaten anytime of day. Below are a list of easy Desserts for everyone to enjoy.

Page Number

86. Chocolate Fudge S'more
87. Banana Bread
88. Brownie
89. Chocolate Chip Mug Cake
90. Chocolate Peanut Butter Mug Cake
91. Microwave Cheesecake
92. Snicker doodle Mug Cake
93. Sticky Date Pudding

Chocolate Fudge S'More

Ingredients

-2 to 3 tbsp Crumbled Graham Crackers
-3 1/2 tbsp Melted Butter
-2 tbsp Sugar
-1 Large Egg
-1/2 tsp Vanilla Extract
-1/4 Cup Whole Wheat Pastry Flour
-2 tbsp Cocoa Powder
-1/8 tsp Baking Powder
-Pinch of Salt
-1 1/2oz Milk Chocolate Chip
-Optional Marshmellow Fluff

Directions

-Combine 3 tbsp Butter, 1oz Chocolate Chips. Melt 20-30 seconds.
- Combine Remaining Butter, Graham Cracker, Stir Til Moist
-Press Graham Cracker Into Bottom of Bowl, Creating Crust
-Whisk Together Egg, Sugar, & Vanilla Til Smooth
-Add In Flour, Baking Powder, Salt, & Cocoa Powder til Batter Forms
-Mix In Melted Butter & Chocolate Mixture.
-Fold In Remaining Chocolate Chips
-Pour Entire Mixture Over Graham Cracker Crust
-Microwave 1 Minute 20 Seconds - 2 Minutes
-Optional Remove & Top With Marshmellow Fluff

Banana Bread

Ingredients

-3 tbsp Flour
-1 tbsp & 1 tsp Sugar
-2 tbsp Brown Sugar
-1/8 tsp Salt
-1/8 tsp Baking Powder
-1/8 tsp Baking Soda
-1 Egg
-1/4 tsp Vanilla Extract
-1 tbsp Vegetable Oil
-1 tbsp Milk
-1 Ripe Banana, Mashed

Directions

-Whisk Flour, Sugar, Salt, Baking Powder, & Baking Soda Together
-Add Egg, Vanilla Extract, Vegetable Oil, Milk, & Mashed Banana
-Spray Microwave Safe Bowl with Non Stick Cooking Spray
-Pour Mixture into Bowl
-Microwave on HIGH for 3 Minutes. Check Every 90 Seconds
- Let Rest Til Cool

Brownie

Ingredients

-2 tbsp Butter
-2 tbsp Sugar
-1 Packet Light Brown Sugar
-1/4 tsp Pure Vanilla Extract
-Pinch Salt
-1 Egg Yolk
-4 tbsp Flour
-1 tbsp Unsweetened Cocoa Powder
-2 tbsp Semi Sweet Chocolate Chips

Directions

-Melt Butter
-Stir Together Butter, Sugar, Vanilla & Salt
-Stir In Egg Yolk
-Add Flour & Cocoa Powder. Stir Until Well Combined
-Add Chocolate Chips
-Microwave 45 Seconds, Til Cooked

Chocolate Chip Mug Cake

Ingredients

-4 tbsp All Purpose Flour
-2 tbsp Brown Sugar
-1/4 tsp Baking Powder
-3 tbsp Low Fat Milk
-1/8 tsp Vanilla Extract
-1/2 tbsp Vegetable Oil
-2 tbsp Semisweet Chocolate Chips

Directions

-Combine Flour, Brown Sugar, Baking Powder, Milk, Vanilla & Vegetable Oil
-Whisk Together Til Smooth
-Whisk In 12 of Chocolate Chips
-Pour Mixture Into Oiled 8oz Mug
-Sprinkle Remaining Chocolate Chips Over Top
-Microwave for 30 seconds til cooked fully
-Let Cool

Chocolate Peanut Butter Mug Cake

Ingredients

-3 tbsp Flour
-2 tbsp Sugar
-1 1/2 tbsp Cocoa Powder
-1/4 tsp Baking Powder
-Pinch of Salt
-3 tbsp Milk
-1 1/2 tbsp Vegetable Oil
-1 tbsp Peanut Butter

Directions

-In 8oz Mug Whisk together Flour, Sugar, Cocoa Powder, & Salt
-Add Milk, Vegetable Oil & Peanut Butter
-Whisk Til Smooth
Microwave Every 30 Seconds til Baked
-Serve After Mixture Lowers & Cools

Microwave Cheesecake

Ingredients

-2oz Cream Cheese
-2 tbsp Sour Cream
-1 Egg
-1/2 tsp Lemon Juice
-1/4 tsp Vanilla Extract
-2 to 4 tbsp Sugar

Directions

-Mix All Ingredients Together In Bowl
-Cook on HIGH for 90 Seconds
-Stir Every 30 Seconds
-Refrigerate Until Served

Snickerdoodle Mug Cake

Ingredients

-1/4 Cup & 2 tbsp All Purpose Flour
-3 tbsp Sugar
-1/4 tsp Baking Powder
-2/4 tsp Cinnamon
-1/4 Cup Milk
-2 tbsp Butter, Melted
-1/2 tsp Vanilla Extract

Directions

-Whisk Together Flour, 2 tbsp Sugar, Baking Powder, 1/4 tsp Cinnamon
-Mix In Milk, Butter & Vanilla til Smooth.
-Combine Remaining Sugar & Cinnamon In Separate Bowl
-Scoop Batter Into Mug. Sprinkling on Cinnamon. Creating Layers
-Microwave on HIGH 1-1 1/2 Minutes
-Continue Cooking Every 30 Seconds Til Baked
-Allow To Cool

Sticky Date Pudding

Ingredients
-10 Dates, Roughly Chopped
-1 1/2 tbsp Boiling Water
-1/8 tbsp Baking Soda
-2 tbsp Butter
-5 1/2 tbsp Brown Sugar
-1 1/2 tbsp Self Raising Flour
-1/2 Egg, Beaten
-1/2 tbsp Walnut, Chopped
-1 Jar Caramel Sauce
-1 tbsp Milk

Directions
- Place Dates & Water in Bowl. Microwave 50 Seconds
-Add Baking Soda. Let Sit 1 Minute
-Mash Dates Roughly With Fork
-Add 1 1/2 tbsp Butter. Melt 10-15 Seconds
-Add 1 1/2 Brown Sugar, Flour, Egg Combine Thoroughly
-Flatten Batter. Sprinkle Walnut on Top

-Microwave 1 Minute
-Cook Every 10 Second Til Cooked
-Let Cook
-Combine Remaining Brown Sugar, Melted Butter, & Milk
-Microwave 20-30 Seconds. Stir
-Repeat Steps 2-3 Times, Til It Looks Like Caramel
-Drizzle Over Top Of Cake

Thank You For Reading This Book. I hope that you the reader either as a Beginner cook, or someone who has limited time has found the recipes to your liking. Hopefully not only have you expanded your cooking abilities but have been able to customize these recipes and expand on the list.

Printed in Great Britain
by Amazon